K. Cat

MW01268720

ENVIRONMENTAL ACTION

Analyze Consider Options Take Action In Our Neighborhoods

WASTE
Reduction

ENVIRONMENTAL ACTION

Analyze Consider Options Take Action In Our Neighborhoods

WASTE
Reduction

A Student Audit of Resource Use

STUDENT EDITION

E2: ENVIRONMENT & EDUCATION

DALE SEYMOUR PUBLICATIONS®
Menlo Park, California

Developed by E2: Environment & Education™, an activity of the Tides Center.

Managing Editor: Cathy Anderson
Senior Editors: Jeri Hayes and Jean Nattkemper
Production/Manufacturing Director: Janet Yearian
Design Manager: Jeff Kelly
Senior Production Coordinator: Alan Noyes
Text and Cover Design: Lynda Banks Design
Art: Rachel Gage, Andrea Reider
Composition: Andrea Reider
Clip Art Illustrations: Copyright © Art Parts, Courtesy Art Parts, 714-834-9166

This book is published by Dale Seymour Publications®,
an imprint of Addison Wesley Longman, Inc.

Dale Seymour Publications
2725 Sand Hill Road
Menlo Park, CA 94025
Customer Service: 800 872-1100

Printed on acid-free,
85% recycled paper
(15% post-consumer).
Printed using soy-based ink.

ISBN 0-201-49537-6
DS30676
1 2 3 4 5 6 7 8 9 10–ML–01 00 99 98 97

CONTENTS

Welcome to Environmental ACTION!

EXPLORE the Issues

ANALYZE

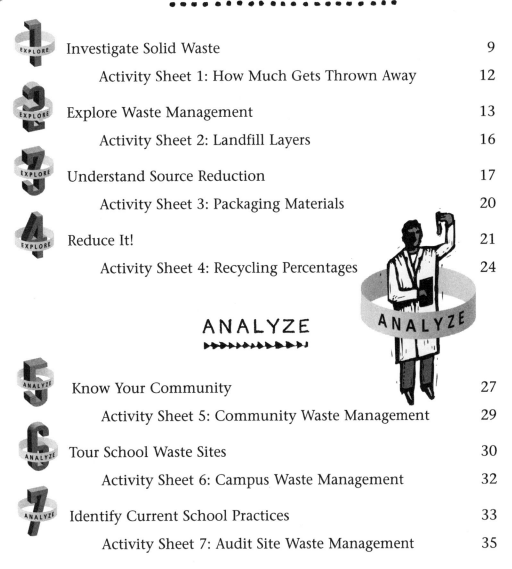

Act Locally
• • • • • • • • •

CONSIDER OPTIONS
▼ ▼ ▼ ▼ ▼ ▼ ▼ ▼ ▼ ▼ ▼ ▼ ▼ ▼ ▼ ▼

Act Locally
• • • • • • • • •

TAKE ACTION

Appendices

Welcome to Environmental ACTION!

Welcome to Environmental ACTION!

This environmental program is designed to give you the knowledge and tools you need to make choices that will improve your quality of life, both now and in the future. You and all other living things modify the environment in order to live. What are the consequences of your actions? What is your impact on other living things and where they live? What is your impact on the food supply, atmosphere, and water cycle? The interrelationships of living things and long-term effects of actions are only beginning to be understood. As human beings, we are unique among earth's organisms because we can choose to change our daily behavior. We can change our actions to reduce our impact on the environment, improve our quality of life, and provide for the needs of future generations. We can conserve and preserve our natural resources.

Using your school as a laboratory, you will investigate environmental issues and analyze how they influence human health and the environment. Each module contains a set of A.C.T. activities that will guide you in your investigations. A.C.T. stands for
- Analyze
- Consider Options
- Take Action

When you have completed your investigation and compiled your research, you will present a proposal for change to your school environmental committee.

What features does a sustainable lifestyle have?

It is renewable. Resources are replaced as they are used.

It is balanced. People and systems work together to improve the environment in the present and ensure the quality of life in the future.

It is manageable. Products are reusable, recyclable, and biodegradable.

Your Journal

Throughout the project, you will be using a Journal. It is a notebook in which you record all your observations and data, write down ideas, make sketches, and outline procedures.

You will need to use your Journal when you are conducting research in a study area, so it should be easy to carry. Your teacher may have specific instructions on what kind of notebook to use.

Action Groups

For most of the activities in this program, you spend part of your time working in a group. Your Action Group will work cooperatively, so that the group members benefit from each other's contributions. Sharing ideas, determining the best steps to take to achieve a goal, and dividing up tasks are just some of the advantages of working together.

Home activities can be done individually, but you may find that you prefer working with a group. Try to include your parents, brothers and sisters, or other family members in your work at home.

Topic Descriptions

The Environmental ACTION project that you are about to begin is one of six modules, or units. Each module focuses on a different aspect of the environment. Your teacher may choose to do only one module, a few modules, or all of the modules. The modules cover the topics discussed below.

Energy Conservation

Using the school as a research laboratory, you'll explore where energy comes from and how it is used, the effect of energy production on the environment, and how to improve energy efficiency at school and at home.

Food Choices

You will investigate the effects of food production, diet, and nutrition on human health and the environment. You will analyze your school's food service programs and identify healthy choices and practices.

Habitat and Biodiversity

You will study the importance of biological diversity, landscape management, xeriscaping, composting, and integrated pest management (IPM). You'll tour the school grounds to assess the current landscaping lay-out and then evaluate the present condition in relation to environmental sustainability. This module also contains a step-by-step guide on how to create an organic garden and a seed bank.

Chemicals: Choosing Wisely

You will investigate the use of hazardous materials—paints, chemical products, cleaning supplies, pesticides—how they are stored and disposed of, and their potential effects on human health and the environment. After evaluating the results, you develop a plan for implementing the use of earth- and human-friendly alternatives at school and home.

Waste Reduction

After you sort your school's garbage to identify recyclable and compostable materials and analyze the school's current waste practices, you will formulate a plan to reduce your consumption and waste at school and at home. Development or improvement of a recycling program may be part of the process.

Water Conservation

After an introduction to water consumption and water-quality issues, you'll conduct an audit of water usage and efficiency to determine whether current consumption practices on campus can be improved. You will then develop strategies for implementing water conservation at school and home.

Explore the Issues

INVESTIGATE SOLID WASTE

EXPLORE

What to do with solid waste is a big problem. But before we can figure out what to do with solid waste, we need to know what it is. Find out about solid waste: what is in it, how much there is worldwide, and what Americans typically throw away.

Setting the Stage

Discuss these questions:

1. What is solid waste?

2. What kinds of solid waste do you throw away in a typical week?

3. What happens to solid waste after you throw it away?

Vocabulary

Did you know fact

compost, composted
incinerate, incineration
landfill
recycle
solid waste

... Temple of the Sun at Teotihuacan in Mexico and over twenty-five times the size of the Great Pyramid of Khufu at Giza in Egypt.

William Rathje & Cullen Murphy, *Rubbish!*, Adapted from *The Archaeology of Garbage*, HarperCollins, 1992, p. 4

Focus

A. Study the diagram on p. 10, and then discuss the questions. Solid waste includes all items disposed of in landfills, incinerated, recycled, or composted. It does not include sewage or items put down a garbage disposal. You may wish to read more about solid waste in Issues and Information section A.

EXPLORE

Paper 50%

Plastic 2%

Metal 7%

Yard Debris 15%

Food 10%

Glass 8%

Other 8%

1. Which material gets thrown away most often in our trash cans?

2. What materials do you think are included in the category "Other"?

3. What would be the reduction in solid waste if all yard wastes and food wastes were composted?

B. Complete all the work on Activity Sheet 1.

It's a Wrap

On a separate sheet of paper or in your Journal, write the answer to each question.

1. Why are we running out of places to dump our solid waste?

2. What are some ways to deal with our solid waste problem?

Home

In your Journal, make a chart with the headings shown on page 11.

Time of Day	What I Throw Out	Can it be reused, recycled, or composted?	Is this an item I really need?

Fill in the first two columns by writing what you throw out each day and when you do it. Keep this record for a 24-hour period. Leave the other columns blank. You will fill them in later.

Your teacher will give you a two-part activity sheet like the one below to use with this lesson.

ACTIVITY SHEET

EXPLORE

Name _____

HOW MUCH GETS THROWN AWAY (part 1)

Use the information in the chart below to make a bar graph comparing household waste per person in different countries.

Household Waste in Various Countries

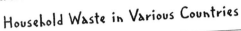

	Yearly House-hold Waste (tons)	Equivalent per person (pounds)
Australia	10,000,000	1500
Canada	12,600,000	1157
Italy	14,041,000	542
Japan	40,225,000	758
Spain	8,028,000	472
Sweden	2,500,000	661
United States	200,000,000	1930

our times as
nuch house-
uch more

[bar graph with y-axis values 2000, 1500, 1000, 500, 0 and x-axis labels: Australia, Canada, Italy, Japan, Spain, Sweden, United States]

1. Which three countries on this list produce the most household waste?

_____

2. Which three countries on this list produce the most household waste per person?

_____

3. Which three countries on this list produce the least household waste per person?

_____

EXPLORE WASTE MANAGEMENT

EXPLORE

Every waste management system has advantages and drawbacks that need to be considered before any one method is implemented. Find out about the positive and negative effects of different waste management systems.

Setting the Stage

Discuss these questions:
1. What is meant by the term "waste management"?
2. What are the different ways that you dispose of waste?

Vocabulary

➤ bacteria   methane
leachate   sanitary landfill

Focus

A. Study the bar graph below and then discuss the questions on p. 14. Material about landfills and other methods of waste management can be found in Issues and Information section B.

Study the questions on p. 14.

THINK ABOUT IT

How long does it take waste materials to decompose in the environment? It takes orange or banana peels 2 years; plastic bags, 15 years; tin cans or leather, 50 years; aluminum cans, 80 years; plastic, an indefinite amount of time.

Adapted from *Foghorn Newsletter*, published by Friends of Gaia, May/June 1991, Vol. III, Number 3.

Waste M a _____ U.S.

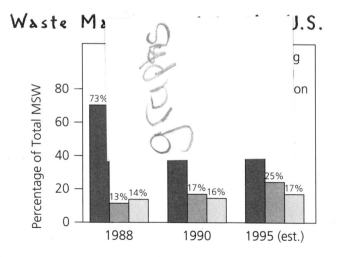

1. What is the most common method of waste management in the U.S.?
2. Which method of waste management almost doubled in use between 1988 and 1995?
3. Which method of waste management is gradually being used more and more?

B. Complete all the work on Activity Sheet 2.

It's a Wrap

On a separate sheet of paper or in your Journal, write a sentence to answer each question.

1. Why do you think use of landfills is declining as a waste management technique?
2. What are some negative effects of incineration of solid waste?
3. Which method of waste management—landfill, incineration, or recycling—is the most environmentally friendly? Explain its benefits.

Home

In your Journal, look at the chart you began in Activity 1. Think about each item you listed as a throwaway. Write an answer for the question in Column 3.

EXPLORE

Time of Day	What I Throw Out	Can it be reused, recycled, or composted?	Is this an item I really need?
7:30 A.M.	uneaten toast		
7:45 A.M.	bird-cage liner		
12:30 P.M.	paper lunch sack plastic sandwich bag apple core aluminum foil wrap- ping for dessert drink carton		

Your teacher will give you a two-part activity sheet
like the one below to use with this lesson.

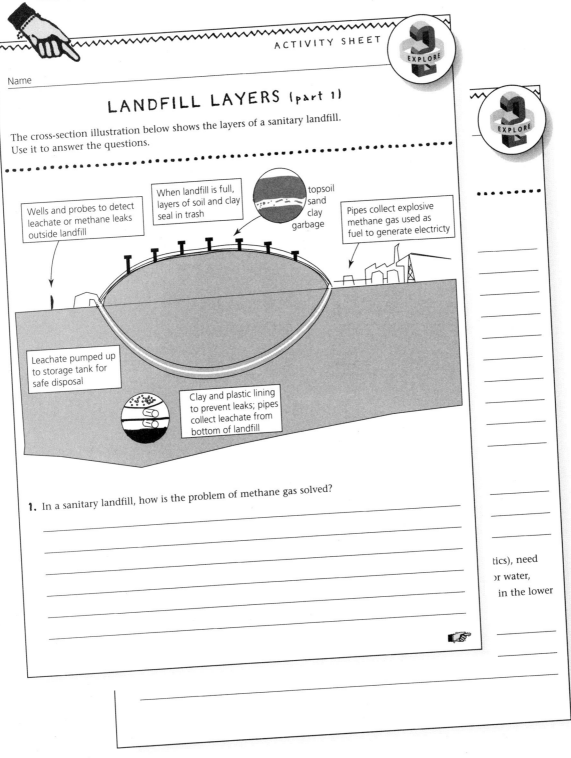

ACTIVITY SHEET

Name _____

LANDFILL LAYERS (part 1)

The cross-section illustration below shows the layers of a sanitary landfill.
Use it to answer the questions.

Wells and probes to detect
leachate or methane leaks
outside landfill

When landfill is full,
layers of soil and clay
seal in trash

topsoil
sand
clay
garbage

Pipes collect explosive
methane gas used as
fuel to generate electricty

Leachate pumped up
to storage tank for
safe disposal

Clay and plastic lining
to prevent leaks; pipes
collect leachate from
bottom of landfill

1. In a sanitary landfill, how is the problem of methane gas solved?

_____

_____

_____

_____

_____

_____

tics), need

or water,

in the lower

UNDERSTAND SOURCE REDUCTION

EXPLORE

Source reduction is one way to control the amount of solid waste that is incinerated or disposed of in a landfill. Source reduction means to cut down both the amount and the toxicity of the waste we produce. Discover ways to practice source reduction and extend the life of the products we use.

Setting the Stage

Discuss these questions:

1. What is source reduction?
2. How can you practice source reduction in your daily life?
3. What are the benefits of practicing source reduction?

Vocabulary

high-density polyethylene (HDPE)
polyethylene terephthalate (PET)
polystyrene, polystyrene foam
source reduction
volume

Focus

A. Study the picture on p. 18, and then discuss the questions. You can learn more about source reduction by reading the material in Issues and Information section C. Material about particular waste items—plastics, paper, yard debris, hazardous wastes—and an example of the life of a product can also be found in Issues and Information.

> ### THINK ABOUT IT
>
> "What's required is a new way of thinking about consumer goods, a challenge to the assumption that everything must inevitably wear out or break and be replaced with a new and improved model, itself destined quickly to wear out or break."
>
> Senator Al Gore, *Earth in the Balance*, Houghton Mifflin, 1992, p. 160

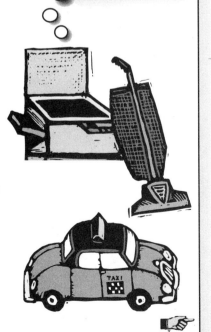

1. What types of packaging are shown in the illustration? Identify the materials that are used.

2. Which of the packaging materials can be reused or recycled?

3. How can the choices that a shopper makes influence the amount of material that is thrown away?

4. How could this shopper purchase the same goods but cut down on waste materials?

B. Complete all the work on Activity Sheet 3.

It's a Wrap

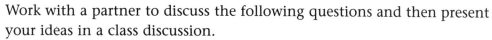

Work with a partner to discuss the following questions and then present your ideas in a class discussion.

1. In a supermarket, what is your response to the question, "Paper or plastic?" Explain your answer.

2. Some people want to replace their clothing at the first sign of wear or fading. They throw out the old clothes and buy new ones. What else could be done with them?

3. Now that you know more about packaging and source reduction, what are some ways you can practice source reduction at school and at home?

Home

In your Journal, look at the chart you have been working on. Make a note of the items that you really need. Then ask yourself how you can practice waste reduction for those items. List your ideas in your Journal.

Time of Day	What I Throw Out	Can it be reused, recycled, or composted?	Is this an item I really need?
7:30 A.M.	uneaten toast	yes—feed to pet or birds, compost	
7:45 A.M.	bird-cage liner	no	
12:30 P.M.	paper lunch sack plastic sandwich bag apple core aluminum foil wrapping for dessert drink carton	reuse or recycle reuse or recycle compost reuse or recycle recycle	

Your teacher will give you a two-part activity sheet
like the one below to use with this lesson.

ACTIVITY SHEET

Name _____

PACKAGING MATERIALS (part 1)

1. It has been estimated that somewhere between one-third and one-half (by volume) of
solid waste we throw out is packaging. List five items that come in packages. For each item,
tell what the package is made of and why it is needed.

_____

_____

_____

_____

_____

_____

_____

_____

_____

_____

_____

2. List three items that do not come in packages. For each item, tell why a package is not needed.

_____

_____

_____

_____

3. Look at the following list of packaging materials. Beside each one, list an item that is packaged
in it. You may wish to look at Issues and Information section F for more about plastics.

- glass_____,_____

- paper or cardboard_____

- steel_____

- aluminum_____

- wood_____

REDUCE IT!

EXPLORE 4

Source reduction is the main way to cut down on the amount of solid waste sent to landfills. Reduction and recycling are two of the 6 Rs. The others are reject, repair, reuse, react. Find out more about how the 6 Rs can be used to reduce waste.

Setting the Stage

Discuss these questions:

1. What are some ways to reduce the amount of waste material we throw out?

2. Why is it important to reduce the amount of waste material we throw out?

3. What items that you use regularly can be recycled?

Vocabulary

ferrous
pre-consumer
post-consumer
6 Rs

Focus

A. Study the chart on page 22, and then discuss the questions. Material about recycling can be found in Issues and Information section D.

1. Approximately what percentage of our aluminum is recycled?

2. Which material is recycled the least?

3. About how much of our paper and paperboard is not recycled?

Percentage of Produced Materials That Are Recycled in the U.S.

(data from Environmental Protection Agency, 1993)

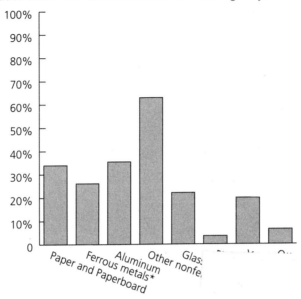

*Ferrous metals are those metals that contain some iron. Ca¹ ferrous metals.

B. The 6 Rs stand for six words that describ¹ material. Discuss the 6 Rs: *reject, reduce,* *react.* How do they relate to source reduction: For example, you might reject buying a certain item because of the way it is packaged.

C. Complete all the work on Activity Sheet 4.

It's a Wrap

Working with a partner or small group, design a poster or think of bumper sticker slogans to promote the 6 Rs. You can highlight the benefits of one of the 6 Rs, or you can explain what or how to use it. Share your ideas with the rest of the class.

Home
. . . . .

In your Journal, look back at the chart you have been working on. Look at the items you identified as being reusable or recyclable. Circle those that are recyclable. Then briefly describe how you or your family would recycle each item you circled. Would you put it by the curb for weekly pickup, take it to a recycling center, deposit it in a special bin in the front of a supermarket, or would you need to do some investigating to find out how to recycle it?

Time of Day	What I Throw Out	Can it be reused, recycled, or composted?	Is this an item I really need?	Could source reduction have prevented the whole problem?
7:30 A.M.	uneaten toast	yes—it can be fed to pet or wild birds or composted	yes	yes—shouldn't cook more than I can eat
7:45 A.M.	bird-cage liner	no	yes	no
12:30 P.M.	paper lunch sack plastic sandwich bag apple core aluminum foil wrapping for dessert drink carton	lunch sack and plastic sandwich bag are reusable; apple core can be composted; aluminum can be reused or recycled; drink carton can be recycled	need the food, but do not need some of the packaging	yes—sandwich can be packed in a reusable container; apple core can be composted; dessert can be packed in a reusable container

Your teacher will give you a two-part activity sheet
like the one below to use with this lesson.

Name

RECYCLING PERCENTAGES (part 1)

Make three pie charts from the information provided below. Use the following key to color the
sections of your charts: recycled or reused—green; waste-to-energy—yellow; disposed of in a
landfill or "other"—brown. Then use the charts to answer the questions.

Solid Waste Management in Three Countries (percentages)

Source	United States	Japan	West Germany
Recycled or reused	11	50	15
Waste-to-Energy	6	23	30
Landfilled or Other	83	27	55
Total	100	100	100

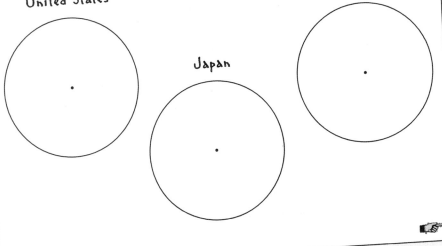

tegories

note the

s.

lations

Analyze

KNOW YOUR COMMUNITY

ANALYZE

To give you an overview of what is happening in your community, a local resource person will come to your class to discuss local waste management issues. Use this opportunity to obtain as much specific information as you can about what happens to waste materials in your community.

Setting the Stage

Discuss these questions:

1. What kinds of wastes are generated in your community?

2. Where and how are they disposed of?

3. What are the problems associated with the current waste management system in your community?

4. What plans are being considered to improve the current waste management system in your community?

Vocabulary

waste management system

Focus

Use Activity Sheet 5 as a guide when you find out about waste management in your community and ask questions about how waste is disposed of. Use the chart to record information.

Be sure to find out about programs for reuse and recycling that are available in your community.

THINK ABOUT IT

Many believe that because socioeconomic factors play a large part in the placement of hazardous waste dumps, sewage treatment plants, and waste incinerators, poor and minority communities suffer disproportionate exposure to environmental and health risks. This belief has given rise to the environmental justice movement.

adapted from "Environmental Justice: Win, Lose, or Draw?" by Deb Starkey, *State Legislatures*, March 1994,

▼ ▼

It's a Wrap

Review the information you recorded on Activity Sheet 5. In your Journal, write a paragraph describing how the speaker helped you understand some aspect of waste management in your community.

Home

Interview someone in your home about waste management. Find out all you can about how garbage is collected where you live. Where is it picked up? How often? Where is it taken? Record this and other information in your Journal.

Your teacher will give you a two-part activity sheet
like the one below to use with this lesson.

Name

COMMUNITY WASTE
MANAGEMENT (part 1)

Use this sheet to record information as you listen to the presentation by the local
resource person(s). If any questions occur to you during the presentation, jot them
in the margin or on the back of this sheet and ask the speaker at the appropriate time.

Name of Speaker: ⎯⎯⎯⎯⎯⎯⎯⎯⎯⎯⎯⎯⎯⎯⎯⎯⎯⎯⎯⎯⎯

Speaker's Place of Employment: ⎯⎯⎯⎯⎯⎯⎯⎯⎯⎯⎯⎯⎯⎯⎯
⎯⎯⎯⎯⎯⎯⎯⎯⎯⎯⎯⎯⎯⎯⎯⎯⎯⎯⎯⎯⎯⎯⎯⎯⎯⎯⎯⎯⎯⎯

Speaker's Job Title and Responsibilities: ⎯⎯⎯⎯⎯⎯⎯⎯⎯⎯
⎯⎯⎯⎯⎯⎯⎯⎯⎯⎯⎯⎯⎯⎯⎯⎯⎯⎯⎯⎯⎯⎯⎯⎯⎯⎯⎯⎯⎯⎯

Topic of Presentation: ⎯⎯⎯⎯⎯⎯⎯⎯⎯⎯⎯⎯⎯⎯⎯⎯⎯⎯⎯
⎯⎯⎯⎯⎯⎯⎯⎯⎯⎯⎯⎯⎯⎯⎯⎯⎯⎯⎯⎯⎯⎯⎯⎯⎯⎯⎯⎯⎯⎯

Main Ideas:

Current Programs for Handling Waste Materials:

TOUR SCHOOL WASTE SITES

ANALYZE

To give you an overview of how waste materials are handled at your school, a school resource person will discuss campus waste management issues and take you on a campus tour. As you walk through the school with the speaker, notice the various places where waste materials are collected.

Setting the Stage

Discuss these questions:

1. What types of wastes are generated on campus?
2. How are waste materials collected and removed from the school?
3. Are any of the waste materials being recycled or handled in some other special way? Describe them.
4. How many different kinds of collection sites are there? Describe them.

Focus

As you listen to the resource person, record information and answers to questions in the appropriate section of Activity Sheet 6.

It is important that you pay attention to and observe safety precautions throughout the course of the module. Your teacher will explain the school policy and procedures that you are to follow.

As you visit different areas, look for places where waste material is collected. Think about the following:

1. How many waste containers are in this area?
2. What kind of containers are used?
3. What kind of waste material is put into the containers in this area?
4. Are any of the containers marked for recycling or any other special handling? If so, describe their use.

THINK ABOUT IT

"If today is a typical day on planet earth, humans will add fifteen million tons of carbon to the atmosphere, destroy 115 square miles of tropical rainforest, create seventy-two square miles of desert, eliminate between forty to one hundred species, erode seventy-one million tons of topsoil, add twenty-seven hundred tons of CFCs to the stratosphere, and increase their population by 263,000."

David Orr,
Ecological Literacy
(Albany: State University of New York Press, 1992), p. 3

It's a Wrap

Discuss your work on Activity Sheet 6. Add or change items as you receive feedback and suggestions from classmates. In your Journal, write a short paragraph describing how the tour helped you find out about how waste is handled on campus, what waste items if any are recycled, and where collection sites are located.

Home

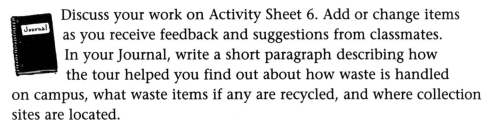
In your Journal, make a chart that shows the locations of waste containers and recycling bins in your home.

Your teacher will give you a two-part activity sheet
like the one below to use with this lesson.

ACTIVITY SHEET

ANALYZE

Name _____

CAMPUS WASTE MANAGEMENT

Record information you learn from meeting with the resource person and touring the school.

Part 1: Preparing for the Tour

Name of Speaker: _____

Speaker's Job Title and Responsibilities: _____

_____

1. How are waste materials collected at school? (Include as much information as you can
about the work of the clean-up crews and waste collection agency.)

_____

_____

_____

_____

2. Are any of the waste materials being recycled or handled in any other special way?
If so, describe them.

_____

_____

_____

_____

3. What safety precautions should you observe when investigating separated waste
materials on campus?

_____

_____

_____

☞

of Recycling
r Method of
Reduction

IDENTIFY CURRENT SCHOOL PRACTICES

ANALYZE

In this lesson the class will be divided into Action Groups to prepare for a Waste Management Audit. Each Action Group will be responsible for at least one audit site and will work closely with a supervisor in charge of that area.

Setting the Stage

Discuss these questions:

1. Where is waste material collected at school?
2. What waste-related data can you gather at each waste collection site?
3. How can all the sites be covered most efficiently?

Focus

A. Think about what you learned on the campus tour and the information you recorded on Activity Sheet 6. As a class, brainstorm all areas of the school where waste material is collected. List the places on the chalkboard. (Note: Restrooms will not be part of the audit.)

B. Look at the chart on the chalkboard. Can you think of other areas that should be included? If so, add them now.

C. Your teacher will divide the class into Action Groups and assign at least one audit site to each group. Once your Action Group is formed, you will need to get together and plan your audit strategy.

D. Complete the work on Part I of Activity Sheet 7.

E. Arrange for a special tour of your audit site with the supervisor in charge of the area. Complete the work on Part II of Activity Sheet 7.

> ### THINK ABOUT IT
> Almost four million computer diskettes are thrown away every day, which equals over one and a half billion disks per year or a stack of disks as tall as the Sears Tower in Chicago every 21 seconds. It will take nearly 500 years for the disks to degrade.
>
> adapted from GreenDisk/Diskette Recycling Program flyer

It's a Wrap

In your Journal, write a paragraph that describes current waste management practices at each of your audit sites.

Home

In your Journal, write a paragraph that describes current waste management practices in your home.

Your teacher will give you a two-part activity sheet like the one below to use with this lesson.

7
ANALYZE

Name _____

AUDIT SITE WASTE MANAGEMENT

Part 1: Prepare to Visit Your Audit Site

Action Group: _____
_____

Audit Site (Area of Responsibility): _____
_____

Supervisor of Audit Site: _____
_____

Meet with the supervisor at each of your audit sites. Explain that you need to record data about current waste management at the particular campus site. Arrange a time to meet with your supervisor to tour the audit site. Record information about the site provided by the supervisor. Include any safety precautions or other considerations and concerns that you should pay special attention to as you conduct your audit.

_____
_____
_____
_____
_____
_____

What else do you need to know before you conduct your audit?

_____
_____
_____
_____

☞

7
ANALYZE

r example,
ny other
bout the
er.

2. What other observations about waste management did you make?

_____
_____

COLLECT WASTE MATERIALS

ANALYZE

Your Action Group collected general information about current waste management at various school sites. Your group will now plan how to audit the sites to determine the amount and type of waste material collected.

Setting the Stage

Discuss these questions:

1. How can you gather data about the amount of materi̇ thrown away at your waste site on a given school dȧ

2. Why is it important to sort materials that are throw away?

3. How should materials be sorted?

4. What will your Action Group need to do in order to gather information?

Focus

A. Use what you have learned and observed to brainstorm a list of waste materials you are likely to find on the school campus. Sort the materials into categories, such as paper, plastic, aluminum. Determine whether you can find subcategories for the materials. For example, subcategories for paper might include computer paper, art paper, newspaper, cardboard, waxed cartons, magazines, and so on. Note whether or not an item can be recycled or reused. How can the categories you choose help you find ways to reduce waste at the source?

B. Work together with your Action Group to complete Activity Sheet 8. Note that you will need to contact your audit area supervisor to go over your plans for this second part of your Waste Management Audit.

C. Discuss your ideas with others in the class to see if your methods of sorting and collecting will yield results that can be used later, when data from all the Action Groups is compiled.

THINK ABOUT IT

In the United States, 28 billion bottles and jars are collected for recycling every year.

̇ass saves

̇w

̇g

̇es

̇er to light a ̇ bulb for up to four hours.

adapted from *50 Simple Things Kids Can Do To Save The Earth*, The Earth Works Group, p. 23

Side bear

D. You will be setting out labeled containers to collect waste material for analysis. Consider the following questions and choose someone from your Action Group to make sure that each task is completed.

1. What labels will you need for the containers?

2. Who will create the labels and place them on the containers?

3. Where will the containers be placed?

4. Will you need more containers? If so, how many?

5. Where will you get more containers if you need them?

6. How much does each container hold? To find the volume of a cylinder, use a tape measure or ruler to measure its diameter and its height. Multiply π (3.1416) times the radius (one-half the diameter) times the height: πrh. To find the volume of a square or rectangular container, multiply length times height times width (l×h×w). Note that some containers and bags or liners that fit them may be labeled with standard sizes expressed in gallons or cubic feet.

7. What kinds of signs will be needed in the audit area? Who will create them? When will they be put up?

It's a Wrap

Discuss the information you recorded on the activity sheet, along with any questions you have. You may wish to add to the information you gathered. In your Journal, write a paragraph about your Action Group's audit plan. Use information from Activity Sheet 8 to describe the steps you will take to conduct your audit.

Home

Plan a Waste Management Audit of your home. Start by recording the kinds and amounts of waste material that are disposed of on any given day. You can then use that data to project what will be disposed of over a week, month, or year. In your Journal, describe your plans for conducting a home audit and make a chart that can be used to collect data.

Analyze: Collect Waste Materials   **37**

Your teacher will give you an activity sheet
like the one below to use with this lesson.

ACTIVITY SHEET

Action Group

ANALYZE

Name

WASTE MATERIALS COLLECTION PLAN

Work with your Action Group to provide the following information.

Audit Site (Area of Responsibility): _____

Audit Site Supervisor: _____

1. What types of waste materials do you expect to find at your audit site? Refer to your notes
on Activity Sheet 7. _____

_____

_____

2. What categories will you use to sort waste materials for your audit?

_____

_____

_____

3. How will you dispose of the waste materials after your audit? _____

_____

_____

_____

4. What safety precautions or other concerns do you need to pay special attention to during
your audit? _____

_____

_____

5. What other information do you need before your audit? You may wish to refer to materials
in Issues and Information. _____

_____

_____

ANALYZE WASTE MATERIALS

ANALYZE

In this activity you will record the amount of material collected in each container at your audit site. Follow your supervisor's instructions to dispose of the material you have collected. When your audit is complete, you will restore the audit site to its original condition.

Setting the Stage

Discuss these questions:

1. What types of materials do you expect to collect at your audit site?

2. What percentage of recyclable materials do you predict you will collect? How might this percentage change depending on the audit site?

Focus

A. Set up the containers at the audit site if you haven't already. Meet with your Action Group and discuss the kinds of waste materials you expect to collect.

B. With your Action Group, look at Activity Sheet 9. Plan to return to the audit site and obtain the data you need to fill in the chart. You may wish to make a checklist to specify tasks that each group member needs to complete.

C. When you return to your audit site, collect the data you need to complete your audit and restore the site to its original condition.

It's a Wrap

Use your observations and inspection of waste materials to create a pie chart to show the kinds of waste materials collected at your site. For example, you might make a pie chart showing the percentage of plastic, paper, and tin or aluminum; a chart showing

THINK ABOUT IT

When considering the impact of plastic in the waste stream, it is important to measure plastic materials by volume and not just weight. Plastics add up to only about 7% of the total waste stream by weight. However, by volume, the contribution of plastic accounts for approximately 30%.

adapted from
Walter H. Corson,
The Global Ecology Handbook,
Beacon Press, 1990, p. 272

the different types of paper collected; or a chart showing the percentage of recyclable, reusable, and nonrecyclable waste materials.

Home

Conduct a Waste Management Audit of your home. On any given day, keep a record of everything that is thrown into the waste containers. Also record amounts of materials that are put into recycling bins. In your Journal, make a chart like the one on Activity Sheet 9.

Your teacher will give you an activity sheet
like the one below to use with this lesson.

ACTIVITY SHEET

Action Group

Name

AUDIT SITE COLLECTION

For each material collected at your audit site, enter the following information.

SAFETY NOTE: This is a visual inspection only. Do not handle any waste materials.

Material Specify the label you put on the container, such as white paper, colored paper, newspaper, aluminum, or any other category you choose for sorting purposes.	Size of Container / Volume For container size/volume, refer to the calculations you made earlier.	Amount of Material Estimate the amount, based on the volume of the container and your own observations.

COMPILE THE DATA

M eet with your Action Group to compile the data collected at your audit site and summarize your observations. Then work with classmates to combine the data of all the Action Groups to get an overall view of what gets thrown away over a given time period at school.

Setting the Stage

Discuss these questions:

1. What have you learned about what gets thrown away at school?
2. What have you learned about how school waste is managed?
3. How can you present the information so that it can easily be understood and interpreted?

Focus

A. Meet with your Action Group. Use the information you gathered during the audit to help you fill in the chart on Part I of Activity Sheet 10. The chart will combine the findings, calculations, and observations of everyone in your group.

B. Using Activity Sheet 10 as a guide, your Action Group can prepare a one-page report specifying the waste material collected at your audit site and describing where it goes.

C. Compare the findings that your group members collected to the summaries that other Action Groups have prepared. Work together to combine the data from all of the audit sites on the chart in Part II of Activity Sheet 10.

> **THINK ABOUT IT**
>
> [The] most preferred type of packaging...is no packaging, followed by minimal packaging, reusable packaging, recycled or recyclable packaging.
>
> adapted from
> Debra Dadd-Redalia,
> *Sustaining the Earth*, p. 55
> and from *Waste: Choices for Communities*, Concern,
> September 1988, p. 13

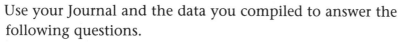

It's a Wrap

Use your Journal and the data you compiled to answer the following questions.

1. What type of waste material is thrown away most often (by volume)? Were you surprised by this finding? Explain your answer.

2. What other observations do you have about waste management at school?

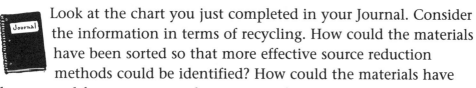

Home

 Look at the chart you just completed in your Journal. Consider the information in terms of recycling. How could the materials have been sorted so that more effective source reduction methods could be identified? How could the materials have been sorted for more comprehensive recycling and reuse? Record your ideas in your Journal.

Your teacher will give you a two-part activity sheet
like the one below to use with this lesson.

ACTIVITY SHEET

Name _____

Action Group

AUDIT SITE DATA (part 1)

Use information collected by your Action Group at your audit site to fill in the chart below.

Waste Collected at Audit Site by Action Group

Date/Time	Container Volume/ Location	Container Label	Waste Material Collected/Volume

ACT LOCALLY

ACT LOCALLY

Now that you have a better understanding of waste management practices, find ways to share what you have learned. Think of a project that will help increase awareness of and involvement in source reduction, or use one of the suggestions given below.

A. Create an article for the school paper or a school-wide flyer featuring a list of source reduction hints that students can follow at school and at home.

B. Join in a community effort such as a paper or can drive, supervised hazardous materials or yard debris collection, or curbside pick-up of recyclable materials that are not part of the weekly recycling program.

C. Plan a school art exhibit featuring items made from 100% post-consumer recycled materials, trash, or products made from recycled materials.

THINK ABOUT IT

[A] large furniture manufacturer, Herman Miller, Inc. (HMI) of Zeeland, Michigan, has reaped savings of $1.4 million annually through waste prevention. It devised packaging containers that can be reused 80 to 100 times and that are made from recycled detergent and milk containers.

adapted from
*The Consumer's Handbook
for Reducing Solid Waste,*
August 1992, p. 29

Consider Options

ASSESS BENEFITS AND COSTS OF WASTE MANAGEMENT

CONSIDER OPTIONS

Review your audit site findings to identify costs and benefits of waste management practices.

Setting the Stage

Discuss these questions:

1. What are the benefits of waste management practices: disposal in a landfill, incineration, composting, recycling?

2. What are the costs of waste management practices— disposal in a landfill, incineration, composting, recycling?

3. What are the costs and benefits of source reduction represented by the 6 Rs?

Vocabulary

 benefit
cost

Focus

A. When you consider waste management practices, you need to think about the costs and benefits. Ask yourself the following questions:

1. What are the monetary costs?
2. What are the nonmonetary costs?
3. What are the hidden costs, if any?
4. What are the benefits to the environment, quality of life, health, and so on?
5. Which of these benefits are immediate?
6. Which of these benefits are long term?

Pose these kinds of questions as you evaluate the waste management practices you observed at your audit site.

> **THINK ABOUT IT**
>
> "Since nothing on earth is inconsequential, use the resources you must with grateful awareness."
>
> From *Inneractions*, by Stephen C. Paul, p. 82 Copyright © 1992 by Stephen C. Paul. Reprinted by permission of HarperCollins Publishers, Inc.

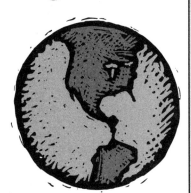

B. Work with a partner and record your observations and assessment on Activity Sheet 11.

It's a W

Review your work on Activity Sheet ~~~~~~~~~~~~~~~~~~up members. Do the benefits of waste~~~~~~~~~~~~~~~~~~sually outweigh the costs? How can th~~~~~~~~~~~~~~~~~~e practices more beneficial in the short an

H~

In your Journal, make a chart simila~ the one on Activity Sheet 11. Identify home waste management practices in terms of benefit and cost.

Your teacher will give you an activity sheet
like the one below to use with this lesson.

Name _____

BENEFITS AND COSTS OF
AUDIT SITE WASTE MANAGEMENT

Audit Site:_____

In the chart below, list waste management practices you observed during your audit, including evidence of source reduction represented by the 6 Rs. Identify the costs and benefits of each practice. Record reasons for your ideas and supporting evidence.

Observation at Audit Site	Benefit/Cost—Reasoning/Evidence

INVESTIGATE SOLUTIONS

CONSIDER OPTIONS

U se what you have learned to identify problems associated with various audit sites and brainstorm ways to solve them. Each Action Group will research the benefits and costs of implementing a particular solution or possible solutions.

Setting the Stage

Discuss these questions:

1. What types of measures can be taken to solve waste management problems?

2. How can the benefits and costs of implementing proposed solutions be estimated?

Focus

A. Brainstorm a list of problems associated with waste management at your audit site.

B. Discuss possible solutions for each problem.

C. Working with your Action Group, research the problems you have identified and find out the costs and benefits of possible solutions.

D. Complete work on Activity Sheet 12.

It's a Wrap

Discuss with your group members the hidden costs and over-riding benefits of your solutions to the waste management problem. Factor any additional observations about benefits and costs into your solution evaluation to include in your presentation later. How can you apply the 6Rs to make solutions more beneficial in the short and long run?

> **THINK ABOUT IT**
>
> "We should all be concerned about the future, because we will have to spend the rest of our lives there."
>
> Charles F. Kettering/*Bartlett's from Seed for Thought* (1949)

Home
· · · · ·

In your Journal, identify problems that you have observed in
how waste is managed in your home. Suggest a number of
possible solutions to the problem and evaluate each one
in terms of costs and benefits.

Your teacher will give you a two-part activity sheet
like the one below to use with this lesson.

ACTIVITY SHEET

Name _____

PROPOSED SOLUTIONS (part 1)

Gather as much information as you can about the problems you are researching
and the solutions you have proposed. Record your findings. You will need more
than one copy of the activity sheet.

Problem: _____
_____

Proposed Solution(s): _____
_____

Source of Information (Identify the person you consult or materials you use to fill in the
information below.) _____
_____

1. What makes the proposed solution feasible? _____
_____

2. How many people are needed to implement the solution? What will their tasks be?
_____
_____
_____
_____

3. How long will it take to implement the plan? _____
How much time will people have to spend each week to accomplish their tasks?
_____
_____
_____

4. What special equipment is needed? _____
_____
_____

ere?

EVALUATE THE RESEARCH

CONSIDER OPTIONS
13

Evaluate the data gathered by each Action Group. Hearing what other groups measured and observed at their audit sites can provide useful information as you consider solutions to waste management problems.

Setting the Stage

Discuss these questions:

1. What information about waste materials and waste management will be useful to my Action Group?
2. Why is it important to weigh the costs and benefits of waste management solutions?

Focus

A. Choose a member of your Action Group to present your waste management solutions to the class. Use the information you provided on Activity Sheet 13.

B. Use the information presented by the Action Groups to fill in Activity Sheet 13. Note which waste management problems match those that you encountered at your site and consider how the proposed solutions compare to your own ideas.

C. After all the presentations have been made, meet with your Action Group to decide which groups provided information that will help you recommend a solution for the waste management problems associated with your audit site. You may wish to ask members of Action Groups additional questions about their solutions to get more details.

It's a Wrap

Think about the information presented by the Action Groups. Choose the three most innovative solutions that you heard, either for the problem identified at your audit site or that of another site.

THINK ABOUT IT

"We're chucking out 10 to 20 billion disposable diapers, two billion razors, 1.7 billion pens, and 45 billion pounds of plastic every year. ...We're now exporting 200 million pounds of it every year—mostly to Asia, where it merely gets landfilled there instead of here."

E Magazine, July/August, 1995, p. 28

Discuss what makes these ideas especially effective. How do your solutions include one or more of the 6 Rs?

Home
•••••

Look at the problems and solutions you have identified for how waste is managed in your home. Using ideas presented by the Action Groups, revise your solutions and re-assess the costs and benefits that will result if the new solutions are implemented. How do your solutions include one or more of the 6 Rs?

Your teacher will give you a two-part activity sheet like the one below to use with this lesson.

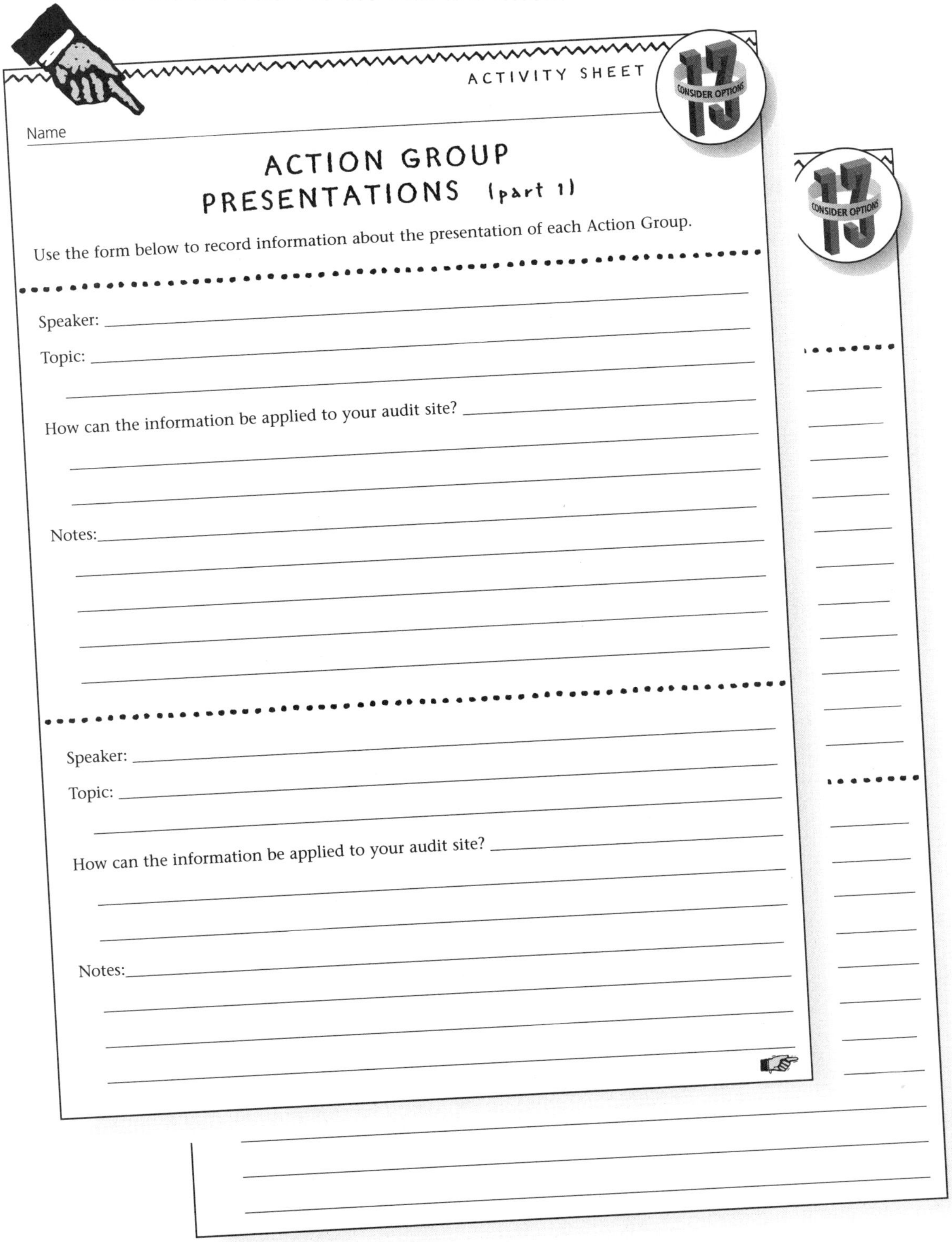
ACTIVITY SHEET 13 CONSIDER OPTIONS

Name

ACTION GROUP PRESENTATIONS (part 1)

Use the form below to record information about the presentation of each Action Group.

Speaker:

Topic:

How can the information be applied to your audit site?

Notes:

Speaker:

Topic:

How can the information be applied to your audit site?

Notes:

ACT LOCALLY

N ow that you have explored a wide variety of waste management and source reduction ideas, share them with your schoolmates by carrying out a project such as the following:

A. Invite parents and students to a panel discussion about waste management systems and source reduction. Include information about source reduction options represented by the 6 Rs.

B. Give a local business or community organization an overview of your Waste Management Audit and the 6 Rs. Suggest ways in which businesses or agencies can promote source reduction in the workplace.

C. Help plan a Reduce Your Waste evening. Invite parents and friends to attend and find out about your waste-management activities.

D. Present your waste management and source reduction information to your school Parent-Teacher group and explain the waste audit being conducted by your Action Groups. The organization may be able to help you implement some of your ideas.

> ### THINK ABOUT IT
>
> "Today we've achieved a finesse
> In packaging goods to excess;
> Using mountains of plastic,
> Foam, nylon—fantastic—
> Tomorrow we'll clean up the mess."
>
> Mrs. Ruth Blandford, *Great Green Limericks*, p. 20

Take Action

MAKE RECOMMENDATIONS

14
TAKE ACTION

Y ou have researched solutions to waste management problems and compared your solutions with those of the other Action Groups in your class. Work with your Action Group to prioritize your solutions and prepare recommendations to present to your classmates for evaluation.

Setting the Stage

Discuss these questions:

1. What do you need to consider in deciding on waste management recommendations for your audit site?
2. What criteria should you use to choose the solutions you will present?
3. What criteria should the class use to choose a recommendation?
4. What features will help make a recommended solution successful?

Focus

Get together with your Action Group and decide on the solutions you will recommend to the class. Give the class a quick overview of your recommendation, explain why you think it is important, and outline what it will take to implement the solutions. Use Activity Sheet 14 to evaluate each Action Group's solutions on a scale of 1 to 3. You may have additional questions that need to be answered before you can reach a consensus on which solutions to propose to the school committee.

> ### THINK ABOUT IT
>
> "I find the great thing in this world is not so much where we stand as in what direction we are moving."
>
> Oliver Wendell Holmes/
> *Bartlett's* from *Autocrat of the Breakfast-Table* (1858)

It's a Wrap

Discuss some of the solutions that earned a low ranking in your evaluation. What factors made you feel that the plans would not be effective? How could the plans have been changed to be more successful over the short and long run?

Home
• • • • •

Present your waste management solutions to your family members. Outline how each person will be expected to participate, how much time it will take, how much it will cost to implement, and how it will benefit the family and the environment over the long run. Family members can use the ranking system to reach a consensus about which measures to adopt.

Your teacher will give you an activity sheet like the one below to use with this lesson.

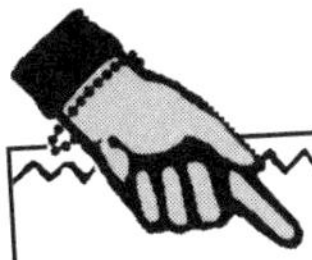

ACTIVITY SHEET

14 TAKE ACTION

Name

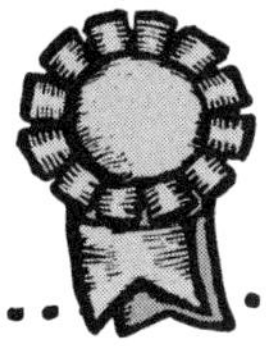

RATING SHEET

Fill in the following ranking sheet for each presentation.

Group

Plan

Costs

Low • • • High

Benefits

Low • • • High

Ease of Implementation

Low • • • High

Cooperation Incentives

Low • • • High

Long-Term Waste Reduction

Low • • • High

Long-Term Source Reduction

Low • • • High

Questions

Assessment

Ranking 1 2 3 4 5

PREPARE AND PRESENT YOUR PROPOSAL

TAKE ACTION 15

You have audited waste management systems at your school, identified areas needing improvement, and determined the solutions that will be most successful on campus. Prioritize solutions presented by the Action Groups and use the ideas to create a proposal to present to the school committee.

Setting the Stage

Discuss these questions:

1. What waste management problems do you want to feature in your presentation?
2. What waste reduction and source reduction measures do you want to emphasize?
3. What approach will make your recommendations for improving waste management systems on campus persuasive and clear?

Focus

A. Think about how you will set up your presentation and decide on what tone your proposal should take. What do you want to emphasize? How can charts, graphs, and tables help you illustrate your ideas? What tone do you think will be most persuasive? Work together to create an outline, using the following as a guideline:

- I. Title
- II. Introduction
   Include a brief summary of the waste materials disposed of at your audit site and the research your Action Group conducted.
- III. Recommendation
   Include information about costs, benefits, step-by-step implementation, increasing awareness and providing opportunities for participation, maintenance, and so on.

> ### THINK ABOUT IT
>
> "We must be the change we wish to see in the world."
>
> Mahatma Gandhi

IV. Research and data
Include facts, figures, projects in the form of illustrations, graphs, charts.

V. Description of beneficial waste management practices already in place at the various audit sites.

B. Use Activity Sheet 15 to manage your preparations.

It's a Wrap

Put together the elements of your proposal and revise parts of it as necessary before delivering it or presenting it to school officials for their consideration.

Home

Write a proposal outlining the waste management solutions your family has agreed to try. Record how each family member will participate in setting up and carrying out the idea.

Your teacher will give you a two-part activity sheet
like the one below to use with this lesson.

ACTIVITY SHEET

Name _____

 PROPOSAL CHECKLIST (part 1)

Use this checklist to plan and monitor tasks that may need to be done in order to
complete your proposal. Make a note of who is responsible for completing each task, when
each task should be completed, materials needed, and so on. Add to the list as needed.

TASKS	NOTES
1. TITLE ☐ Cover illustration ☐ Proposal statement	
2. WRITE THE INTRODUCTORY PARAGRAPH. ☐ Explain the project. ☐ Briefly describe audit results.	
3. WRITE YOUR RECOMMENDATION. ☐ Describe your plan. ☐ Highlight the benefits. ☐ Outline the costs. ☐ Suggest a step-by-step implementation schedule. ☐ Include ideas for motivating student body, increasing awareness, and encouraging participation. ☐ Outline long-range maintenance requirements, costs, planning. ☐ Pinpoint projected savings.	Continue recommendations on next page ☞

explain where you go from here.

FOLLOW UP ON YOUR PROPOSAL

You have presented your waste management recommendation to the school committee, including ways to implement and maintain the plan. Once you find out how your idea was received, you can work to increase awareness and promote the implementation of your proposal.

Setting the Stage

Discuss these questions:

1. How can you discover the effect of your waste management recommendation?
2. How can you judge whether your solutions are working?
3. How can you assess waste management awareness and participation?

Focus

Discuss the waste management proposals that you developed and presented to the committee. How are the solutions being implemented? How can students at your school be challenged to continue to support the waste management plans? How can students be encouraged to consider the 6 Rs as they make decisions as consumers? Use Activity Sheet 16 to summarize the results of your proposals and keep track of progress over time.

It's a Wrap

Discuss how the waste management plans are going. What are the most surprising benefits? What would make the plans more effective? How can you get more people to participate? Keep track of savings as a result of your plan.

Home

Use your Journal to write a progress report about the impact that your waste management plan is having on your household. Explain how it has increased waste management awareness and how family members' habits have changed.

> **THINK ABOUT IT**
>
> "When it comes to the future, there are three kinds of people: those who let it happen, those who make it happen, and those who wonder what happened."
>
> Carol Cristensen

Your teacher will give you a two-part activity sheet
like the one below to use with this lesson.

ACTIVITY SHEET

Name

WASTE MANAGEMENT
TRACKING SHEET (part 1)

Use this tracking sheet to summarize and monitor the results of your proposal
and to assess students' awareness about waste materials and management.

Proposal Summary

Implementation Report

Month 1

Month 2

Month 3

Issues and
Information

SOLID WASTE AND THE SOLID WASTE CRISIS

ISSUES AND INFORMATION

People frequently buy products that they use and throw away, probably without thinking where "away" is or that they are tossing out items of value. We have a throw-away society—we are encouraged to use items quickly and toss them in the trash. But when we do this, we discard natural resources and valuable minerals, and energy. Buried in every landfill are reusable metals and glass, recyclable papers and plastics, and compostable organic waste.

The trash we throw away, other than sewage or garbage that goes down the sink disposal, is called solid waste. This chart shows the composition of municipal and household solid waste in the U.S. Municipal waste is all the waste from households, institutions, and commercial establishments combined.

Material	Composition of U.S. Municipal Waste	Composition of U.S. Household Waste
Paper	40%	50%
Food	7%	10%
Yard	18%	15%
Plastic	8%	2%
Glass	7%	8%
Metals	9%	7%
Other	11%	8%

The U.S. leads the world in trash production—and the amount we produce each year keeps increasing. In 1994, Americans produced 200 million tons of solid waste. That's enough to fill a line of garbage trucks encircling the earth eight times, over half the distance from the earth to the moon. The average person in the U.S. discards about 4 pounds of trash each day, or 1460 pounds per year. Combining all household and industrial waste, every American will throw away 600 times his or her average adult weight in a lifetime.

Where is all this solid waste going? Most of it is dumped in landfills that are rapidly growing—Fresh Kills Landfill on Staten Island in New York will soon be the highest geographic feature between Florida and Maine, a distance of 1500 miles—and filling up. We are running out of places for new landfills, too. Some communities burn their waste as an alternative to using a landfill, but burning solid waste releases harmful air pollutants and leaves behind toxic residue. In fact, all solid waste contains toxic chemicals, whether it is dumped in landfills or incinerated, and the toxins are getting into our water, air, and soil.

As a society, we are faced with a dilemma that many feel is a crisis. What will we do with all our trash? Consider the information listed above. Paper, food, and yard wastes are all recyclable. Recycling instead of throwing away just *half* of those materials would cut municipal solid waste by 33 percent and save valuable resources. Recycling all of it would cut solid waste by almost 70 percent. Changing our behavior can make a big difference. The time for change and for supporting creative solutions to deal with our solid waste crisis is now.

Section B
CURRENT WASTE DISPOSAL

ISSUES AND INFORMATION

This section presents information on two of the most commonly used methods of waste disposal, landfills and incineration. It also gives an overview of a new approach to managing waste disposal, integrated waste management.

Landfills

Most garbage trucks take the garbage to a site where it is dumped and covered by a thin layer of soil. Dump sites used to be uncovered pits or piles. In the 1930s, dump sites started becoming "sanitary landfills" in which a layer of earth is put over the trash to help stop odors, pests, and litter from escaping into the surrounding area. In landfills today, the trash is compacted by bulldozers and other equipment and covered by at least six inches of dirt each day. By law, landfills must be located away from sensitive environments such as streams and rivers, and yet be as close to the source of waste as possible to cut transportation costs. Between 65 and 85 percent of our municipal trash goes to landfills.

Current landfills are filling rapidly—some experts say 80% of the landfills in the U.S. will be filled and closed within the next ten years—and finding sites for new landfills is getting more and more difficult. Solid waste from many communities is already hauled over huge distances—sometimes even to other states or even other countries—to reach a landfill site.

Despite federal monitoring of potential environmental hazards from landfills, there is much evidence that toxins from landfills leak into nearby land and, particularly, into ground water (and from there to drinking water). We are running out of space for landfills not only because of increasing population but also because people are concerned for public health and safety and do not want landfills near their neighborhoods.

Landfills are also expensive. A 100-acre site that would operate for 20 years costs about $87 million, and it can take over five years to get permits and complete development.

Another problem is that waste does not decompose in landfills that are built according to federal regulations. The compacted trash, covered with dirt, especially in areas with low rainfall, is kept airtight and dry. Under these conditions, the bacteria and other organisms that cause decomposition cannot get the oxygen they need to live. The airtight design is intended to keep harmful methane gases (produced when trash does decompose) from escaping into the atmosphere and to prevent leachates from seeping out and contaminating the ground and the water table. But this lack of decomposition is why landfills are filling so quickly. A full trash bag or a stack of newspapers takes up the same amount of space decades after it was first compacted. Researchers have found hot dogs, complete with buns, that have been buried in landfills for forty years.

Incineration

Some communities burn solid waste in huge furnaces. This type of garbage disposal is called incineration. Materials that are incinerated either burn to ash or melt down to residue. About 17 percent of solid waste in the United States is incinerated.

Whether incineration is a good alternative to landfills is a much-debated topic. Here are the arguments for incineration:

- It kills any organisms that could cause disease.
- It reduces the volume of trash by 70% to 90% (all that is left is ash and residue). This reduction is a huge benefit to the landfill problem.
- Energy from the burning can be used as an alternative energy source to produce heat or electricity in what are called waste-to-energy plants. Some countries are using this technique effectively; in the U.S., only 7 percent of trash collected is burned in waste-to-energy plants.
- Although incineration produces toxic air pollution, promoters of incineration state that the emission levels are very low and that waste-to-energy plants would replace other energy-producing plants (such as coal-burning plants) that produce even more pollution.
- It produces little or no potential for pollution of ground water from the incinerator itself.

Here are the arguments against incineration:

- At the end of the burning, toxic ash or residue are left. These toxins are even more concentrated and more easily dissolved in water than they were before burning. Disposing of the toxic residue is itself a waste disposal problem; much of it now goes to landfills where it may leach into soil or ground water.
- Burning produces air pollution containing dangerous vaporized heavy metals—including lead, cadmium, copper, and mercury—and other toxic gases such as nitrous oxide, sulfur dioxide, sulfuric acid, hydrochloric acid, and dioxin. Dioxin, a suspected carcinogen, has been found in the milk of nursing mothers living near incinerators.
- Waste-to-energy incineration plants are extremely expensive to build in the U.S. When voters have been asked to put up tax money to pay for waste-to-energy plants, most have turned them down.
- Opponents claim that because incinerators require huge amounts of trash to burn efficiently, their use discourages attempts to change people's behavior to reduce the amount of trash they generate and recycle. Cities have, in fact, been fined by incineration companies for not providing a promised amount of trash.

Integrated Waste Management

Many communities today are trying to solve the problems of solid waste disposal through integrated waste management—combining the use of all suitable methods of waste disposal in order to change from reliance on landfills and incineration alone. These communities promote have strong recycling programs and encourage people to change behaviors and generate less trash. They try to make landfills and incineration the last, rather than the first, disposal choice. They promote what is called the 6 Rs:
- Reject—don't buy products that are hard to recycle or are wasteful
- Reduce—change how goods are produced and what we buy to reduce the amount and toxicity of trash
- Reuse—substitute reusable items for disposable ones
- Repair—repair damaged goods rather than replacing them
- Recycle—take items to recycling centers to be recycled into new products
- React—let businesses and political leaders know about wasteful or irresponsible waste management practices

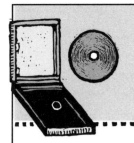

Section C
SOURCE REDUCTION: CONSUMER AND PRODUCER CHOICES

What Is Source Reduction?

Source reduction is perhaps the best solution to waste management problems. Put simply, it means not creating so much waste in the first place. Source reduction includes lowering both the amount and the toxicity of the waste we generate.

Practicing source reduction requires changes in behavior by consumers and by producers of goods. These are some of the aims of source reduction measures:

- to produce and use fewer unnecessary or excessively packaged items
- to lengthen the life span of products
- to make and use nontoxic alternatives to toxic products
- to make products more reusable and recyclable
- to use more recycled materials in the manufacturing of products

Examples of source reduction include consumer choices such as buying only what we really need or using reusable items (such as cups and plates) rather than disposable ones, and manufacturing changes such as making products that last longer or are made of recycled materials.

Packaging

Changing packaging practices is an important method of source reduction. Wrapping and decorating our consumer goods uses a substantial portion of our nation's raw materials: 50 percent of the paper, 8 percent of the steel, 75 percent of the glass, 40 percent of the aluminum, and 30 percent of the plastics. Packaging and containers make up about 33 percent of our solid waste.

Manufacturers compete for our dollars with eye-grabbing packaging that is often much more than is necessary for a product's protection and is often neither recycled nor recyclable. Competition has also led producers to package more products as one-serving, disposable items. Excessive packaging and the short life span of products are steadily increasing the amount of solid waste that must somehow be disposed.

Consumer Choices

What can you as a consumer—or as an advisor to your school or your family—do to help reduce the amount of trash that is created? You can reuse and recycle as much as possible. You can also make careful choices about the products you buy. Other Issues and Information sections will give you more details, but here is a basic checklist of things to ask when making a purchase, so that your choices as a consumer are more environmentally friendly:

1. **Do I really need this product?** Could I borrow or rent it instead? Could I find a used alternative that would serve as well?
2. **How durable is this product?** How long will it last? Long-lasting products cut down on resources used in manufacturing and waste disposal and save you money. Long-lasting light bulbs (such as fluorescents), for instance, save purchase costs, energy costs, and manufacturing resources. For disposable items, look for reusable alternatives.
3. **Is it reusable?** How many times will I be able to use it before discarding it?
4. **Can it be repaired rather than replaced?** Think about whether parts will be available, service repair costs, and whether it would be worth repairing. If not, consider disposal issues.
5. **Is it safe to use?** Choose nontoxic products.
6. **What about the packaging?** Can I buy the item in bulk? Is there another similar product that comes in less packaging? Is the packaging recyclable?
7. **Is it made from recycled or renewable materials?** Look for post-consumer recycled content. Frequently used nonrenewable materials are petroleum and metals.
8. **Are the manufacturing processes used to make it harmless to the environment?** This can be hard to find out, but read labels and try to choose products made from renewable and organically grown materials and products that do not require health or environmental warnings.
9. **Will disposing of it be hazardous to the environment?** Choose safe alternatives to toxic substances.
10. **Can it be disposed of responsibly without being put in the trash?** Look for products that can be recycled, will biodegrade in a compost pile, or can safely be put down the drain.

Making the best choice for the environment is not always easy. For example, if the plastic bag from the grocery store can be used more often and is recycled locally, it might be a better choice than paper. (Of course, using your own reusable bag is best!) Any steps you take, no matter how small, to be a consumer who is sensitive to the environment will have a positive impact.

Section D
RECYCLING AND COMPOSTING

Recycling Has Many Benefits

Every time you recycle an item, you reduce the amount of trash going into landfills or incinerators. You save resources such as metals, trees, water, and energy. You also cut down on the pollution in our air, water, and soil and reduce litter on our land and in our oceans.

Making goods from recycled materials uses much less energy and fewer resources than manufacturing new goods. For instance, making paper from recycled pulp uses over 70 percent less energy and over 50 percent less water than making paper from timber. Twenty aluminum cans can be recycled using the amount of energy it takes to make one new can.

Close the Recycling Loop

Recycling is a three-part loop. It starts with collecting and sorting—you sell or give your used cans, bottles, and paper to a recycling center, business, or community agency. The next step is manufacturing—items are sold and transported from the recycling center to companies that reprocess them and make them into new products. The third step, the step that completes the loop, is when you purchase products that are made from recycled materials.

For recycling to truly work, there must be demand for goods made from recycled materials. If people do not buy these goods, manufacturers won't make them, and the materials collected for recycling may wind up in landfills after all. As consumers, we have the purchasing power that will influence manufacturers to make things from recycled materials. But we need to beware that products labeled "recycled," even "100% recycled," can be made from industrial scraps—waste trimmings from the factories—and do not have to contain any material recycled from previous products. The word to look for is "post-consumer." Post-consumer material is made from products that have already been used by consumers. Pre-consumer material is made from industrial scraps. A product that is labeled as being recycled is a better choice than one that is not, but buying goods with the highest possible post-consumer content truly closes the loop and promotes recycling.

Cozy Sportswear

• Soft and cozy

• Warmer than wool

• Dries quickly

• Made of at least 50% post-consumer recycled polyester

Know Your Materials

Here is information about materials that can commonly be recycled and some of the products that are made from the recycled materials. Find out what can be recycled in your community.

Material	Recyclable Materials	Post-Consumer* Products
Paper	white, colored, glossy, newspaper, brown, cardboard, chipboard	paper products
Food	plant-based scraps and leftovers	compost
Yard debris	leaves, branches, brush, shrub, grass clippings	compost
Plastic	PETE 1 and HDPE 2 are most widely accepted; other types of plastics	bottles, trays, carpet, bags, and fiberfill
Glass		glass, fiberglass, abrasives, construction materials, road paving
Metals	aluminum, steel,	cans, cars, appliances and construction materials
Other	motor oil, paints, toner cartridges	motor oil, paints, toner cartridges

Glass Each year around two billion pounds of glass containers are collected in the U.S. If properly handled, these can be reused by being washed and sterilized. This simple process is used mostly in states that have bottle bills requiring deposits on bottles (deposits are refunded when the bottles are returned). In Oregon, the first state to pass a bottle bill, almost all deposit glass bottles (93%) are recycled.

Most recycled glass is crushed and made into new bottles. Glass that has been treated, however, cannot be recycled, including light bulbs, safety glass, car windows, and baking dishes. Some recyclers require that glass be sorted by color for recycling, but more and more places are now able to take all colors unsorted. Recycling one glass bottle saves enough energy to light a 100-watt bulb for four hours. Only 22% of the glass produced in the U.S. in 1993 was recycled.

Aluminum Cans Aluminum cans are the most easily and efficiently recycled of all recyclable products. It is a lot less expensive for manu-facturers to make new cans from old ones than to make them from new materials—and saves 95 percent of the energy used. The average can that is recycled is back on the shelf in about six weeks. We are recycling about half of our aluminum cans now. That's good, but we are still throwing away over a million tons of aluminum each year.

Tin and Steel We use about 100 million tin and steel cans a day in the U.S., such as tuna and pet food cans. Although these cans are recy-clable, we throw away enough steel to build all the new cars in the U.S. each year. Every pound of steel recycled saves over 5000 Btu's of energy—that's enough to light a 60-watt bulb for more than 26 hours.

New, recycled steel is produced from melting steel scrap taken from appliances, automobiles, and other products. In 1993, enough appliances were recycled to build 214 Olympic stadiums and enough steel from old cars was recycled to produce almost 12 million new automobiles.

Yard and Food Wastes Composting yard and food wastes is the way to recycle them—nature's way. It is the process of decomposition of organic material— yard clippings, leaves, and kitchen scraps—into nutrient-rich matter that can be used by plants and animals. Bacteria, fungi, and other organisms are the decomposers that break down the organic matter. Food and yard wastes make up at least 25 percent of U.S. household trash, all of which could be composted. A simple back-yard compost pile—or a community composting center—can turn this organic waste into usable soil. It is estimated that over three million U.S. families are composting today.

Paper and Plastic Sections F and H give you more information about paper and plastic.

Other Materials: Motor Oil, Toner Cartridges, and Paints Motor oil can be re-refined into good, reusable oil. However, only 3 percent of the 1.35 billion gallons of used oil generated each year in the U.S. gets recycled. As much as 30 percent of it is improperly dumped into sewers and landfills. Recycling oil helps waste disposal problems and saves this scarce, nonrenewable resource. Recycle your used motor oil (at service stations and community centers) and buy re-refined oil.

Similarly, toner cartridges (which supply the ink for copy machines and computer printers) and many paints can be recycled. Like motor oil, they are made from petroleum products, so not recycling them adds to our waste disposal problems and uses scarce petroleum resources.

A Special Case: Recycling Videocassettes In 1994, more than 900 million videocassettes were produced in the United States; less than 1% were recycled. Most of the major parts of videocassettes are recyclable, with the exception of some of the material in the magnetic tape. Petroleum, a nonrenewable energy resource, is used in making both the tape case and the magnetic tape (one half-inch VHS tape requires about one-sixth gallon of petroleum to produce). There are three ways that companies recycle videocassettes: used tapes are erased and reused; damaged tape is replaced with new or erased tape; or tapes are removed and the plastic cases converted into other products. You can help efforts to recycle videocassettes both by taking your cassettes to a recycler and by buying recycled ones.

How Are We Doing At Recycling?

The chart on p. 84 shows how much we are recycling of different materials in the U.S. Although there has been an encouraging increase in how much we are recycling in recent years, there's plenty of room for improvement.

RECYCLING IN THE UNITED STATES, 1993

Material	Millions of tons generated	Millions of tons recycled	% of generated that is recycled
Paper & Paperboard	77.8	26.5	34.0%
Ferrous metals	12.9	3.4	26.1%
Aluminum	3.0	1.1	35.4%
Other nonferrous metals	1.2	0.8	62.9%
Glass	13.7	3.0	22.0%
Plastic	19.3	0.7	3.5%
Yard Wastes	32.8	6.5	19.8%
Other	46.2	3.0	6.5%
Total	206.9	45.0	21.7%

WHAT YOU CAN DO TO HELP REDUCE SOLID WASTE

ISSUES AND INFORMATION

We each make choices every day about products we buy. We also make choices about how we dispose of the trash we generate. Below you will find some buying and disposal practices that will help reduce the amount and toxicity of our solid waste.

Shop for the Environment

- Buy only what you need.
- Avoid over-packaged products.
- Buy in bulk.
- Avoid single-use and disposable items such as razors, diapers, cups, plates.
- Avoid nonrecyclable and one-use packaging such as mixed-material plastics, juice boxes, blister packs.
- Buy items in packaging that can be recycled in your community (find out what can be recycled).
- Buy refillable bottles of milk, soft drinks, and other beverages.
- Buy rechargeable batteries and solar-powered calculators.
- Avoid toxic products (such as some furniture polishes, drain cleaners, bath and kitchen cleaners, silver and copper cleaners, pesticides).
- Read labels to determine potential hazards.
- Grow fruits and vegetables without using toxic chemicals.
- Buy organic produce.
- Buy "old-fashioned" cleaners like baking soda, borax, lemon juice, and vinegar.
- Buy pure beeswax furniture polish.
- Buy pump sprays rather than aerosol cans.
- Avoid detergents or cleaners containing phosphates; buy vegetable-based soaps instead.
- Avoid chlorine-based scouring powders.
- Buy fluorescent rather than incandescent bulbs; they last many times longer and use less energy.

- Buy products with recycled content (the higher the post-consumer recycled content, the better) such as gray paperboard boxes, recycled paper, envelopes, paper towels, tissues, napkins; also clothing, shoes, and building materials made from recycled materials.

*Read the information on making choices as a consumer in Section C.

Don't Throw It Away**

- Compost food and yard waste.
- Recycle whenever possible; be up-to-date on your community's recycling program and on special services such as plastic bag recycling bins at supermarkets and motor oil, tire, and antifreeze recycling at gas stations.
- Know what hazardous wastes are and dispose of them properly.

**Read the information on recycling, composting and disposing of hazardous materials in Sections D, F, and G.

Choose To Reuse

- Paper bags — bring your own to reuse at the grocery store (small and large)
- Coat hangers and plastic bags from the cleaners — return for reuse
- Foam peanuts and bubble wrap — take to packaging stores for reuse or save and reuse for your next package
- Clothing, furniture, appliances, toys — donate to charitable organizations
- Dishes and cups — take your own to work or school to use instead of paper
- Paper — reuse paper printed on one side as scrap paper; copy on both sides
- Greeting cards — reuse the front part as a post card
- Magazines and books — give to someone else to read; donate to a hospital, school, or library
- Gift wrap — save it to reuse on smaller packages
- Old bedding, drapes, clothing — cut into pieces for rags
- Mailing envelopes — attach a new mailing label and reuse

Some more ideas for reusable alternatives to disposable products are:

Disposable	Reusable
Aluminum foil	Baking pans
Batteries	Rechargeable batteries
Lunch bags (paper or plastic)	Metal, plastic, or cloth reusable lunch box or bag
Paper coffee filters	Cloth or metal mesh filters
Paper napkins	Cloth napkins
Paper or plastic grocery bags	Cloth tote bags
Paper plates and cups	China, pottery, glass, or plastic plates and cups
Paper towels	Cloth towels, rags, sponges
Plastic flatware	Stainless steel or silver flatware
Plastic food wrap	Jars, bottles, and plastic product packaging
Plastic produce bags	Reuseable polyester mesh bags, paper bags
Plastic lighters or matches	Refillable lighters
Plastic pens	Refillable fountain or ballpoint pens
Plastic razors	Refillable or electric razors
Tissues	Cloth handkerchiefs

Section F
PLASTICS

ISSUES AND INFORMATION

These are the common plastics, including their recycle codes, whether or not they can be easily recycled, and some of the recycled products made from them:

CHARACTERISTICS OF COMMON PLASTICS

Type	Properties	Uses	Recycle Code	% Recycled	Recycled Products Made
PET (PETE) polyethylene terephthalate	tough, shatter-resistant, resistant to chemicals and gases	soft drink, detergent, cooking oil, and juice bottles	**1** commonly recycled	24.6% bottles; 23.2% packaging	carpets, fabric, fiberfill, non-food containers
HDPE high density polyethylene	tough, flexible, translucent	milk jugs, milk and soft drink crates, pipe, plastic grocery bags	**2** commonly recycled	6.3% packaging; 3.6% overall	motor oil bottles, detergent bottles, pipes, pails
PVC polyvinyl chloride; V vinyl	strong, clear, brittle unless treated with plasticizers	luggage, pipes, auto parts, shampoo bottles, shrink wrap, records, hoses	**3** rarely recyclable	0.2% packaging; 0.1% overall	drainage pipes, fencing, house siding
LDPE low density polyethylene	moisture-proof, inert	trash bags, squeeze bottles, diaper liners, cellophane wrap	**4** sometimes recyclable	1.0% packaging; 0.5% overall	trash bags, pallets

Type	Properties	Uses	Recycle Code	% Recycled	Recycled Products Made
PP polypropylene	light, stiff, resistant to heat and chemicals	auto battery cases, screw-on caps and lids, yogurt and margarine tubs, pipes	**5** rarely recyclable	0.4% packaging; 2.2% overall	auto parts, batteries, carpets
PS polystyrene	brittle, rigid; resistant to heat and cold	coffee cups, egg cartons, packaging pellets, carry-out containers	**6** difficult to recycle	1.2% packaging; 0.5% overall	insulation board, office equipment, reusable cafeteria trays

Plastics have become more popular in the United States every year, and for good reason. They are tough, durable, flexible, waterproof, transparent, and can be shaped into a seemingly limitless number of products. But plastics present quite a set of problems.

One problem is that plastics are made from oil, a nonrenewable resource whose supply is running out quickly. Every time we throw away something made of plastic, we are wasting this resource. Another is that plastics littering our land and oceans are harmful to wildlife. Sea turtles, for example, die from eating polystyrene foam mistaken for food. Birds and fish get caught in plastic netting and the plastic rings from beverage six-packs.

Disposing of plastics is a big problem. Currently, they are taking up huge amounts of space in landfills—some studies estimate up to 32 percent of the landfill space. Furthermore, most of them do not decompose: cups made of polystyrene (sometimes called by one of its trademark names, Styrofoam) will still be polystyrene cups 500 years from now. Even so-called "degradable" plastics do not biodegrade; they only break down into smaller pieces. If plastics are incinerated, they produce toxic gases and residues (PVC plastic produces especially hazardous residue when burned). And finally, although some plastics can now be recycled, there are many different types and some products contain more than one type. Knowing how to recycle them can be confusing.

There are encouraging parts to the plastics story, though. Refillable PETE bottles are gaining popularity for soft drinks. Deposits of 8 to 50 cents are required on them which are refunded when they are returned. Some of the bottles are now averaging 20 uses and represent 20 to 40 percent of sales of certain beverages. Also, two plastics—PETE (or PET) and HDPE are easily melted down and recycled. PETE is the most commonly used plastic, mostly for soft drink bottles and food containers. HDPE is used for such items as milk bottles and grocery bags. People are recycling these plastics, which are being made into such diverse recycled products as carpets, paint brushes, drain pipes, and trash cans. The recycling of these plastics is promising, and new technologies for recycling other plastics are being developed every day. Currently, however, in the U.S. less than 4 percent of the plastics we produce are being recycled.

Source reduction is the best solution to the plastics problems. Don't buy unnecessary plastics. For instance, avoid products packaged in plastic that are designed to be used only once and thrown away. React! Let companies know that you don't want their products packaged in needless, excessive plastic packaging. When you do buy plastics, don't buy plastics that cannot be recycled. Look on the bottom of plastic containers—you will find a recycling symbol (a circle or triangle of arrows) with the recycle code inside it. Sort plastics by these codes and turn them in for recycling.

#1

PETE

Section G
HOUSEHOLD
HAZARDOUS WASTES

ISSUES AND INFORMATION

Hazardous wastes are wastes that are toxic and potentially damaging to the environment and to our health. Each year in the United States almost 300 million tons of hazardous waste are generated—that's over one ton per person—and much of it is from products we use in our homes. About one percent of household garbage is estimated to be composed of hazardous compounds. We don't think of our homes as full of toxic products, but take a look at the lists on page 92 to get an idea of what products are hazardous and how to dispose of them safely.

Toxic products cause many accidental poisonings each year from improper handling in our homes. They also cause problems on a larger scale because people do not dispose of them properly. They are often illegally poured down drains or discarded into landfills; from there, they contaminate ground water, surface water, and soil. In communities where garbage is incinerated, the burning of these dangerous wastes can release a toxic mixture of gases and heavy metals (such as lead, mercury, and nickel). These dangerous pollutants can cause lung problems, cancer, birth defects, and other serious health problems. Hazardous wastes thrown into the trash can also be directly harmful to the trash collectors and landfill workers who have to handle them.

Urban run-off is another way that household hazardous wastes get into the environment. Water that makes its way into the gutters along the street and from there into the city's drain system is urban run-off. It may contain toxic soaps from washing a car, herbicides from water that sprinkled a lawn, or thoughtlessly discarded oil from a car oil change. Some of the potentially hazardous materials in urban run-off are animal wastes, pesticides and herbicides, leaking oil and gasoline from parked cars, and swimming pool cleaners.

Not using hazardous materials in the first place is the best way to solve the problem of their disposal. Shop for and use safe alternatives. But when you do have hazardous products to get rid of, dispose of them safely. Find out about hazardous waste collection in your community (call your city or county health and safety departments). The waste collection agency in your area may even be able to recycle some of the common household hazardous wastes. Always call your city officials or your community sanitation company if you aren't sure how to dispose of something safely.

SAFE DISPOSAL OF HOUSEHOLD HAZARDOUS WASTES

A Materials: Must be disposed of through a community collection program or a licensed hazardous wastes contractor (cannot be put down the drain or in the garbage).

B Materials: Can be thrown away with household trash if they are sealed in a closed container and identified (cannot be poured down the drain).

C Materials: Can be diluted with water and poured down the drain.

A Materials	B Materials	C Materials
auto batteries	aerosol cans (empty)	alcohol-based lotions (perfumes, aftershaves)
automatic transmission fluid	auto body repair products	aluminum cleaners
battery acid	cutting oil	ammonia-based cleaners
brake fluid	fertilizer	antifreeze
bug sprays	nail polish	bathroom cleaners
car wax	oven cleaners	disinfectants
diesel fuel	paint (oil-based)	drain cleaners
floor care products	shoe polish	hair permanent lotions
fuel oil		hair relaxers
fungicide		medicines
furniture polish		paint (latex)
gasoline		paint brush cleaner with TSP
glue		paint primer
herbicide		photographic chemicals
insecticide		window cleaner
kerosene		windshield washer solution
lighter fluid		
mercury batteries		
metal polish		
moth balls		
motor oil		
paint (auto, model)		
paint brush cleaner with solvent		
paint stripper		
paint thinner		
rat poison		
weed killer		

ISSUES AND INFORMATION

Consider the following facts about paper:

- Paper and paper products account for close to 50 percent of the solid waste disposed of in the U.S.
- 70 million tons of raw paper are manufactured in the U.S. every year.
- People in the U.S. annually consume over 6 times as much paper per person as the average world citizen.
- An estimated 100 billion trees are cut annually to produce paper products.
- Paper can take just as long as plastic to decompose in compacted landfills.
- All forms of paper are easily recycled.
- Recycling the papers from one Sunday edition of the New York Times would save an estimated 75,000 trees.
- About 20 million tons of paper are recycled annually in the U.S.—less than 30% of the amount produced.

Most of us are aware of the fact that we use a lot of paper and that billions of trees are being cut down to make paper. Most of us know that paper can be recycled and that we need to recycle more of it. But fewer people are aware that there are other problems with paper and ink as well.

First, clear cutting is often used to obtain trees for paper manufacture. Clear cutting strips a forested area of every tree regardless of whether it is usable, leaving the land devastated and vulnerable to erosion.

Second, the paper manufacturing process uses a lot of water and a lot of energy. Paper manufacture uses more fuel oil than any other U.S. industry and is the third largest industrial user of electricity and coal. The burning of these fossil fuels (oil and coal) emits sulfur dioxide and nitrogen oxides, which are the main causes of acid rain.

Third, most paper manufacturing involves the use of chlorine bleaches and other harmful chemicals. These chemicals—which are linked to serious health problems—are discharged into the air and, especially, into streams and rivers. One study has shown that 900,000 tons of toxic pollutants are released in waste water from paper plants each year.

Even the paper recycling can create toxic emissions in the processing required to get rid of ink and bleach paper white.

The inks we commonly use are made with petroleum, a nonrenewable resource. As the inks dry, the petroleum evaporates, releasing dangerous gases into the air.

What's the solution? As with most environmental issues, solutions to the problems posed by paper and ink require a combination of measures, including changes in our behavior as consumers and waste-disposers, as well as changes in the paper and ink industries. Here are some of the solutions to the problems posed by paper and ink:

- **Recycle all paper and paper products.** If we recycled all our paper products, we would cut our municipal waste in half! Making recycled paper uses far less water and energy than making paper from new timber.
- **Buy recycled paper and paper products (including writing paper, printing paper, paper towels, bath tissue).** Choose recycled, unbleached ~~~~ ~t been "de-inked" and has the highest post-consu~ `` It is usually gray or tan with darker flec~ determine whether paper is really rec~ i a school district purchases 300 case~)0% post-consumer paper, it would ~ ⌐5,000 kilowatts of energy, 220 pounds of a~ ⌐d 11 cubic yards of landfill space.
- **Practice source reductio~** er. For example, copy on both sides of paper; reuse paper, e~ ⌐pes, and boxes; and make notepads out of scraps of paper.
- **Buy paper from sources other than trees.** (See below.)
- **Buy soy-based inks.** (See below.)
- **Cut only trees grown in sustainable managed forests.** Cut only those trees that are managed and harvested in a manner that promotes the long life of the forest and a diversity of life in the forest.

Recycled or Not?

We need to be careful consumers in our choice of recycled paper. The chasing arrows recycle symbol was developed for paper, but paper can be labeled "recycled" and contain very little recycled content. Learn to read the information under the recycle label and choose paper in terms of "pre-consumer" and "post-consumer" fibers. Post-consumer fiber means what we generally think of as recycled: the fibers have been recycled from fibers used by consumers before us. Pre-consumer fiber, on the other hand, is fiber that comes from industrial scraps—sometimes just waste trimmings swept from the floor of the paper plant. Using pre-consumer fiber does save some resources, but it doesn't help put back to use the paper we put in recycle bins. Choose paper products with the highest post-consumer content. Its use has the greatest impact in reducing solid waste.

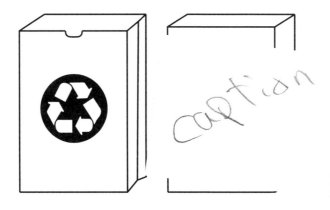

caption

Treeless Paper Sources

Ninety-nine percent of the paper produced in North America is made from wood. We have the knowledge and technology to produce paper from a number of other sources which would require far less land and save our natural forests. The U.S. Department of Agriculture estimates, for example, that 10,000 acres of hemp would produce as much paper as 40,000 acres of trees. Many countries are making paper from various other sources. These are some alternatives to using tree pulp for making paper.

Bamboo Bamboo has especially strong fibers which, in India, are blended with the more-available rice straw to make strong pulp for paper. Bamboo pulp for paper is also produced in Vietnam, Brazil, Bangladesh, and Thailand.

Cereal straws from rice, wheat, oats, barley, and rye "Waste" straw left after the harvesting of the grain can be made into paper. China, India, Pakistan and Spain use cereal straws to make paper.

Hemp Hemp was used to make paper in the U.S. until the early 1900s. It is a very fast-growing plant with strong fibers suitable for paper. Brazil has been growing hemp for paper since the 1960s. Hemp is also grown for paper and paper products in the former Soviet states, Eastern Europe, France, and China.

Kenaf The bark or the stalk of the kenaf plant can be used to make paper. It is a quickly-growing plant—it takes about 150 days to mature to 15 feet in height. Its use to replace wood pulp for paper is being investigated in the southern U.S. and Japan.

Sugar cane The stalks left after the juice is extracted from sugarcane, called bagasse, are used to make pulp for paper. In 1992, two million metric tons of bagasse pulp were produced for paper. Mexico and Peru each produced about 300,000 tons.

Soy Ink

Besides using recycled paper, it is important to consider the type of ink used on the paper. Soy ink is a good alternative to environmentally harmful conventional inks. Soy ink is made with soybean oil, a renewable, nontoxic ingredient (the same oil found in salad oil and mayonnaise). While the drying of conventional inks produces a 25% to 40% rating of harmful emissions, the drying of soy ink produces less than 10% (from the pigments, not from the oil). Paper recycling is faster and produces better quality recycled paper when soy inks have been used. The reason for this is that soy ink can be removed more easily and quickly from the paper pulp, thereby causing less damage to the fibers. Presently soy inks are used to print about 90% of America's daily newspapers.

Section I
A LIFE CYCLE ASSESSMENT FOR A REAL PRODUCT

When considering whether to purchase a product, it would be ideal if we considered the environmental impact of the entire life cycle of the product including its manufacture, use, and disposal. Manufacturers do such assessments, but as consumers we rarely see them. A life cycle assessment looks at all the resources—materials, water, and energy—used in the product's manufacture; any pollutants or hazardous wastes produced; and the impact of the product's disposal at the end of its life. With information like this on every product, we as consumers could certainly make environmentally sound choices. This section gives an example of an actual life cycle assessment of Arm & Hammer Baking Soda.

Baking Soda Life Cycle

Product Description Baking soda is 100 percent pure sodium bicarbonate ($NaHCO_3$), a natural inorganic sodium salt; a white crystalline powder, odorless, slightly salt taste; when heated, it gives off carbon dioxide. Low toxicity. Not classified as a health hazard.

Product Manufacture Made from processed trona ore mined in southwestern Wyoming.

Packaging Packaged in cartons made of 57% post-consumer and 38% pre-consumer recycled paperboard with 5% clay coating material. Inks used are food-safe.

Use and Reuse A multi-purpose product used for baking. Also used as a drain freshener, laundry additive, surface cleaner, cat litter deodorant, refrigerator/freezer deodorant, toothpaste. It is used once and then discarded, except after use as a refrigerator/freezer deodorant (it can then be used as a drain freshener).

Transportation Vehicles are used as part of trona mining to transport the raw materials to the manufacturing facilities; to transport packaged baking soda to stores and households; and to transport manufacturing, distribution, and post-consumer wastes to landfills and incineration facilities.

Waste Management Waste from the refi~ ~re: Shale, clay, and silica are pumped into ponds ? ~ nonhazardous solid waste.

Manufacturing Wastes Bakin~ ~ ~andfill.

**Baking soda disposed of by consu~ ~andfill, incinerated, or dissolved and pou~ ~.

Baking soda packaging Can be recycl~ ~posed of in a landfill, or incinerated.

Environmental Impact of Baking Soda Life Cycle

Waste Water No adverse waste water releases associated with household uses.

Air Pollution Carbon dioxide emissions are 1400 pounds per ton of baking soda used; carbon dioxide, a greenhouse gas, is mostly due to the manufacturing process and transportation. Other emissions average less than 10 pounds per ton of baking soda used.

Solid Waste 80 percent of baking soda in household use is disposed of down the drain, which creates fewer environmental problems than disposal in a landfill. Not associated with the production of any significant hazardous waste.

Conclusions The results of this study indicate that baking soda is environmentally harmless.

Dadd-Redalia, Debra. *Sustaining the Earth.* New York: Hearst Books, pp. 57–61. Courtesy of Church & Dwight Company, Inc.

GLOSSARY

bacteria (pl.) tiny organisms; some cause disease, some help matter decompose

benefit any waste management practice that has a beneficial effect on the environment, on public health, and on financial cost; includes alternative practices, services, and products

compost, composted (n.) mixutre of decaying organic matter, such as plant material; (v.) to make into compost

cost any waste management practice that has a negative effect on the environment, on public health, and on financial cost

decompose to cause to rot

ferrous containing iron

high-density polyethylene (HDPE) plastic used for milk and juice jugs, containers for detergents, shopping bags; recycled (type 2) to make pipes, playground equipment

incinerate, incineration to burn completely

landfill solid waste disposal in which trash is buried between layers of dirt

leachate liquid that percolates or drains through porous material

methane odorless, colorless, flammable natural gas; important source of hydrogen

polyethylene terephthalate (PET) plastic used to make soft drink bottles; recycled (type 1) to make carpeting, egg cartons, garbage cans, insulation for ski jackets

polystyrene, polystyrene foam rigid, clear plastic or foam plastic (Styrofoam)

post-consumer product made from a material recycled by a consumer

pre-consumer product made from a material from scrap or other source

recycle to take out useful materials and reuse or reprocess them

sanitary landfill see landfill; dump site that has been cleaned up and can be used

6 Rs consumer practices aimed at waste reduction: reject, reduce, reuse, repair, recycle, react

solid waste waste that does not include sewage or organic materials put down a garbage disposal

source reduction effectively reducing the amount of material that becomes garbage

volume space or capacity expressed in cubic units

waste management system combination of methods practiced to reduce, reuse, recycle, and dispose of waste material

waste stream various types of waste; may be tracked form collection to disposal in landfill or other destination